The Human Body in Symbolism

By
Manly P. Hall

Copyright © 2022 Lamp of Trismegistus. All rights reserved. No part of this publication may be reproduced or transmitted in any form or by any means, electronic or mechanical, including photocopying, recording, or by any information storage and retrieval system, without permission in writing from Lamp of Trismegistus. Reviewers may quote brief passages.

ISBN: 978-1-63118-609-7

Esoteric Classics

Other Books in this Series and Related Titles

Aurora of the Philosophers by Paracelsus (978-1-63118-507-6)

Rosicrucian Rules, Secret Signs, Codes and Symbols by various (978-1-63118-488-8)

On the Philadelphian Gold by Philochrysus & Philadelphus (978-1-63118-511-3)

Paracelsus, the Four Elements and Their Spirits by M P Hall (978-1-63118-400-0)

The Stone of the Philosophers by A E Waite (978-1-63118-509-0)

Clairvoyance and Psychic Abilities by A Besant &c (978-1-63118-403-1)

The Rosicrucian Chemical Marriage by Christian Rosenkreuz (978-1-63118-458-1)

The Alchemical Catechism of Paracelsus by Paracelsus (978-1-63118-513-7)

Alchemy in the Nineteenth Century by Helena P. Blavatsky (978-1-63118-446-8)

Rosicrucians and Speculative Masonry in the Seventeenth Century (978-1-63118-489-5)

Qabbalistic Teachings and the Tree of Life by M P Hall (978-1-63118-482-6)

The Sepher Yetzirah and the Qabalah by M P Hall (978-1-63118-481-9)

The Devil in Love by Jacques Cazotte (978–1–63118–499–4)

Fortune-Telling with Dice by Astra Cielo (978-1-63118-466-6)

History, Analysis and Secret Tradition of the Tarot by Hall &c (978-1-63118-445-1)

Crystal Vision Through Crystal Gazing by Frater Achad (978-1-63118-455-0)

The Golden Verses of Pythagoras: Five Translations (978-1-63118-479-6)

Arcane Formulas or Mental Alchemy by W W Atkinson (978-1-63118-459-8)

The Machinery of the Mind by Dion Fortune (978-1-63118-451-2)

The A E Waite Reader: A Selection of Occult Essays (978-1-63118-515-1)

The Leadbeater Reader: A Selection of Occult Essays (978-1-63118-483-3)

Audio versions are also available on Audible, Amazon and Apple

Other Books in this Series and Related Titles

Masonic and Rosicrucian History by M P Hall & H Voorhis (978-1-63118-486-4)

The Kabbalah of Masonry & Related Writings by E Levi &c (978-1-63118-453-6)

Some Deeper Aspects of Masonic Symbolism by A E Waite (978-1-63118-461-1)

Masonic Symbolism of King Solomon's Temple by A Mackey &c (978-1-63118-442-0)

The Old Past Master by Carl H Claudy (978-1-63118-464-2)

The Influence of Pythagoras on Freemasonry and Other Essays (978-1-63118-404-8)

The Mysteries of Freemasonry & the Druids by various (978-1-63118-444-4)

The Book of Wisdom of Solomon by King Solomon (978-1-63118-502-1)

The Two Great Pillars of Boaz and Jachin by A Mackey &c (978-1-63118-433-8)

The Regius Poem or Halliwell Manuscript by King Solomon (978-1-63118-447-5)

The Lost Keys of Freemasonry or The Secret of Hiram Abiff (978-1-63118-427-7)

The Master Mason's Handbook by J S M Ward (978-1-63118-474-1)

Brothers & Builders by Joseph Fort Newton (978-1-63118-506-9)

Symbolism and Discourses on the Entered Apprentice, Fellowcraft and Master Mason Blue Lodge Degrees by various (978-1-63118-413-0)

Freemasonry in the Medieval or Middle Ages by various (978-1-63118-450-5)

American Indian Freemasonry by A C Parker (978-1-63118-460-4)

Freemasonry, Mithraism and the Ancient Mysteries by various (978-1-63118-407-9)

The Ceremony of Initiation: Analysis & Commentary (978-1-63118-473-4)

The Symbols and Legends of Masonry by C H Vail (978-1-63118-504-5)

The Janeites, The Man Who Would Be King and Other Stories of Freemasonry by Rudyard Kipling (978-1-63118-480-2)

Audio Versions are also available on Audible, Amazon and Apple

Table of Contents

Introduction...7

Human Body in Symbolism...9

INTRODUCTION

The word "esoteric" can be difficult to define. Esotericism in general can be seen less as a system of beliefs and more as a category, which encompasses numerous, different systems of beliefs. It's a bit of juxtaposition, since the word "esoteric" indicates something that few people know about, while the term itself broadly covers numerous philosophies, practices, areas of study and belief systems.

In a greater sense, Esotericism acts as a storehouse for secret knowledge, which is often considered ancient (by *tradition, if not by fact*), passed down from generation to generation, in private. At various times in history, simply possessing the knowledge of some of these subjects, was considered illegal and a jailable offence, if discovered. This usually included such general topics as Alchemy, Pharmacology, Qabalah, Hermeticism, Occultism, Ceremonial Magic, Astrology, Divination, Rosicrucianism and so on. Collectively, these areas of study were often referred to as the esoteric sciences.

Sometimes, the outer garment of a subject isn't esoteric, while what is hidden beneath it, is. As an example, Freemasonry isn't necessarily esoteric by nature (at *least not anymore*), but certain signs, passwords and handshakes given to the candidate during their initiation, are in fact, esoteric, in the sense that they are hidden from the general public.

Today, in the twenty-first century, such topics are readily available at bookstores across the country, and numerous main-steam publishers offer beginners guides and coffee-table volumes on many of these subjects, intended for mass appeal. Books like *"The Secret"* have turned previously arcane topics into household knowledge. All that being the case, however, it isn't to say that there still aren't buried secrets to uncover, ancient wisdom being ignored and forgotten mysteries to be explored. In fact, it is often that we are only able to further our own studies by standing on the shoulders of these disappearing giants.

Lamp of Trismegistus is doing its part to help preserve humanity's esoteric history by making some of these classics available to those students who are seeking to unearth the knowledge of these ancient colossi.

So, be sure to check other titles from our *Esoteric Classics* series, as well as our *Occult Fiction, Theosophical Classics, Foundations of Freemasonry Series, Supernatural Fiction, Paranormal Research Series, Studies in Buddhism* and our *Christian Apocrypha Series*. You can also download the audio versions of most of these titles from Amazon, Apple or Audible, for learning on the go.

THE HUMAN BODY IN SYMBOLISM

THE oldest, the most profound, the most universal of all symbols is the human body. The Greeks, Persians, Egyptians, and Hindus considered a philosophical analysis of man's triune nature to be an indispensable part of ethical and religious training. The Mysteries of every nation taught that the laws, elements, and powers of the universe were epitomized in the human constitution; that everything which existed outside of man had its analogue within man. The universe, being immeasurable in its immensity and inconceivable in its profundity, was beyond mortal estimation. Even the gods themselves could comprehend but a part of the inaccessible glory which was their source. When temporarily permeated with divine enthusiasm, man may transcend for a brief moment the limitations of his own personality and behold in part that celestial effulgence in which all creation is bathed. But even in his periods of greatest illumination man is incapable of imprinting upon the substance of his rational soul a perfect image of the multiform expression of celestial activity.

Recognizing the futility of attempting to cope intellectually with that which transcends the comprehension of the rational faculties, the early philosophers turned their attention from the inconceivable Divinity to man himself, with in the narrow confines of whose nature they found manifested all the mysteries of the external spheres. As the natural outgrowth of this practice there was fabricated a secret theological system in which God was considered as the Grand Man and, conversely, man as the little god. Continuing this analogy, the universe was regarded as a man and, conversely, man as a miniature universe. The greater universe was termed the *Macrocosm*--the Great World or Body--and the Divine Life or spiritual entity controlling its functions was called the *Macroprosophus*. Man's body, or the individual human universe, was termed the *Microcosm*, and the Divine Life or spiritual entity controlling its functions was called the *Microprosophus*. The pagan Mysteries were primarily concerned with instructing neophytes in the true relationship existing between the *Macrocosm* and the *Microcosm*--in other words, between God and man. Accordingly, the key to these analogies between the organs and functions of the *Microcosmic* man and those of the *Macrocosmic*Man constituted the most prized possession of the early initiates.

In *Isis Unveiled*, H. P. Blavatsky summarizes the pagan concept of man as follows: "Man is a little world--a microcosm inside the great universe. Like a fetus, he is suspended, by all his *three* spirits, in the matrix of the macrocosmos; and while his terrestrial body is in constant sympathy with its parent earth, his astral soul lives in unison with the sidereal *anima mundi*. He is in it, as it is in him, for the world-pervading element fills all space, and is space itself, only shoreless and infinite. As to his third spirit, the divine, what is it but an infinitesimal ray, one of the countless radiations proceeding directly from the Highest Cause--the Spiritual Light of the World? This is the trinity of organic and inorganic nature--the spiritual and the physical, which are three in one, and of which Proclus says that 'The first monad is the Eternal God; the second, eternity; the third, the paradigm, or pattern of the universe;' the three constituting the Intelligible Triad."

Long before the introduction of idolatry into religion, the early priests caused the statue of a man to be placed in the sanctuary of the temple. This human figure symbolized the Divine Power in all its intricate manifestations. Thus the priests of antiquity accepted man as their textbook, and through the study of him learned to understand the greater and more abstruse mysteries of the celestial scheme of which they were a part. It is not improbable that this mysterious figure standing over the primitive altars was made in the nature of a manikin and, like certain emblematic hands in the Mystery schools, was covered with either carved or painted hieroglyphs. The statue may have opened, thus showing the relative positions of the organs, bones, muscles, nerves, and other parts. After ages of research, the manikin became a mass of intricate hieroglyphs and symbolic figures. Every part had its secret meaning. The measurements formed a basic standard by means of which it was possible to measure all parts of cosmos. It was a glorious composite emblem of all the knowledge possessed by the sages and hierophants.

Then came the age of idolatry. The Mysteries decayed from within. The secrets were lost and none knew the identity of the mysterious man who stood over the altar. It was remembered only that the figure was a sacred and glorious symbol of the Universal Power, and it finally came to be looked upon as a god--the One in whose image man was made. Having lost the knowledge of the purpose for which the manikin was originally constructed, the priests worshiped this effigy until at last their lack of spiritual understanding brought the temple down in ruins about their heads and the statue crumbled with the civilization that had forgotten its meaning.

Proceeding from this assumption of the first theologians that man is actually fashioned in the image of God, the initiated minds of past ages erected the stupendous structure of theology upon the foundation of the human body. The religious world of today is almost totally ignorant of the fact that the science of biology is the fountainhead of its doctrines and tenets. Many of the codes and laws believed by modern divines to have been direct revelations from Divinity are in reality the fruitage of ages of patient delving into the intricacies of the human constitution and the infinite wonders revealed by such a study.

In nearly all the sacred books of the world can be traced an anatomical analogy. This is most evident in their creation myths. Anyone familiar with embryology and obstetrics will have no difficulty in recognizing the basis of the allegory concerning Adam and Eve and the Garden of Eden, the nine degrees of the Eleusinian Mysteries, and the Brahmanic legend of Vishnu's incarnations. The story of the Universal Egg, the Scandinavian myth of Ginnungagap (the dark cleft in space in which the seed of the world is sown), and the use of the fish as the emblem of the paternal generative power--all show the true origin of theological speculation. The philosophers of antiquity realized that man himself was the key to the riddle of life, for he was the living image of the Divine Plan, and in future ages humanity also will come to realize more fully the solemn import of those ancient words: "The proper study of mankind is man."

Both God and man have a twofold constitution, of which the superior part is invisible and the inferior visible. In both there is also an intermediary sphere, marking the point where these visible and invisible natures meet. As the spiritual nature of God controls His objective universal form-which is actually a crystallized idea--so the spiritual nature of man is the invisible cause and controlling power of his visible material personality. Thus it is evident that the spirit of man bears the same relationship to his material body that God bears to the objective universe. The Mysteries taught that spirit, or life, was anterior to form and that what is anterior includes all that is posterior to itself. Spirit being anterior to form, form is therefore included within the realm of spirit. It is also a popular statement or belief that man's spirit is within his body. According to the conclusions of philosophy and theology, however, this belief is erroneous, for spirit first circumscribes an area and then manifests within it. Philosophically speaking, form, being a part of spirit, is within spirit; but: spirit is more than the sum of form, As the material nature of man is therefore within the sum of spirit, so the Universal Nature, including the entire sidereal system, is within the all-pervading essence of God--the Universal Spirit.

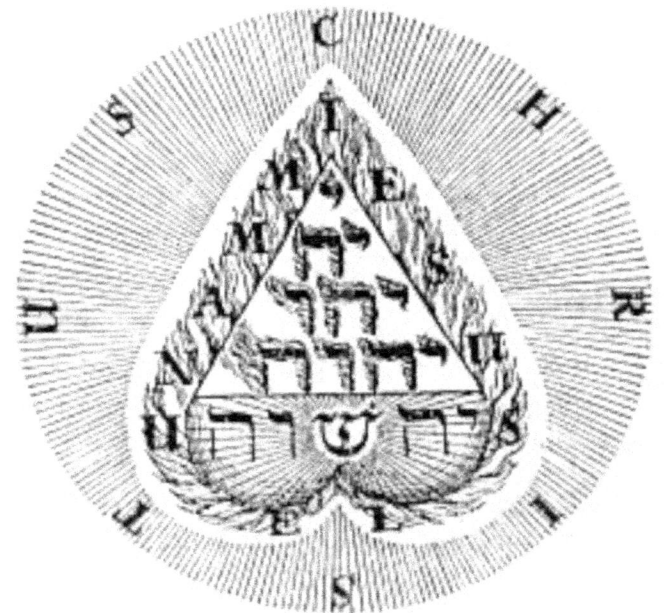

THE TETRAGRAMMATON IN THE HUMAN HEART[1]

---

[1] From Böhme's *Libri Apologetici*.

The Tetragrammaton, or four-lettered Name of God, is here arranged as a tetractys within the inverted human heart. Beneath, the name *Jehovah* is shown transformed into *Jehoshua* by the interpolation of the radiant Hebrew letter שׁ, *Shin*. The drawing as a whole represents the throne of God and His hierarchies within the heart of man. In the first book of his *Libri Apologetici*, Jakob Böhme thus describes the meaning of the symbol: "For we men have one book in common which points to God. Each has it within himself, which is the priceless Name of God. Its letters are the flames of His love, which He out of His heart in the priceless Name of Jesus has

According to another concept of the ancient wisdom, all bodies--whether spiritual or material--have three centers, called by the Greeks the *upper* center, the *middle* center, and the *lower* center. An apparent ambiguity will here be noted. To diagram or symbolize adequately abstract mental verities is impossible, for the diagrammatic representation of one aspect of metaphysical relationships may be an actual contradiction of some other aspect. While that which is above is generally considered superior in dignity and power, in reality that which is in the center is superior and anterior to both that which is said to be above and that which is said to be below. Therefore, it must be said that the first--which is considered as being above--is actually in the center, while both of the others (which are said to be either above or below) are actually beneath. This point can be further simplified if the reader will consider *above* as indicating degree of proximity to source and *below* as indicating degree of distance from source, source being posited in the actual center and relative distance being the various points along the radii from the center toward the circumference. In matters pertaining to philosophy and theology, *up* may be considered as toward the center and *down* as toward the circumference. Center is spirit; circumference is matter. Therefore, *up* is toward spirit along an ascending scale of spirituality; *down* is toward matter along an ascending scale of materiality. The latter concept is partly expressed by the apex of a cone which, when viewed from above, is seen as a point in the exact center of the circumference formed by the base of the cone.

---

revealed in us. Read these letters in your hearts and spirits and you have books enough. All the writings of the children of God direct you unto that one book, for therein lie all the treasures of wisdom. * * * This book is Christ in you."

These three universal centers--the one above, the one below, and the link uniting them-represent three suns or three aspects of one sun--centers of effulgence. These also have their analogues in the three grand centers of the human body, which, like the physical universe, is a Demiurgic fabrication. "The first of these [suns]," says Thomas Taylor, "is analogous to light when viewed subsisting in its fountain the sun; the second to the light immediately proceeding from the sun; and the third to the splendour communicated to other natures by this light."

Since the superior (or spiritual) center is in the midst of the other two, its analogue in the physical body is the heart--the most spiritual and mysterious organ in the human body. The second center (or the link between the superior and inferior worlds) is elevated to the position of greatest physical dignity--the brain. The third (or lower) center is relegated to the position of least physical dignity but greatest physical importance--the generative system. Thus the heart is symbolically the source of life; the brain the link by which, through rational intelligence, life and form are united; and the generative system--or infernal creator--the source of that power by which physical organisms are produced. The ideals and aspirations of the individual depend largely upon which of these three centers of power predominates in scope and activity of expression. In the materialist the lower center is the strongest, in the intellectualist the higher center; but in the initiate the middle center--by bathing the two extremes in a flood of spiritual effulgence--controls wholesomely both the mind and the body.

As light bears witness of life-which is its source-so the mind bears witness of the spirit, and activity in a still lower plane bears witness of intelligence. Thus the mind bears witness of the heart, while the generative system, in turn, bears witness of the mind.

Accordingly, the spiritual nature is most commonly symbolized by a heart; the intellectual power by an opened eye, symbolizing the pineal gland or Cyclopean eye, which is the two-faced Janus of the pagan Mysteries; and the generative system by a flower, a staff, a cup, or a hand.

While all the Mysteries recognized the heart as the center of spiritual consciousness, they often purposely ignored this concept and used the heart in its exoteric sense as the symbol of the emotional nature, In this arrangement the generative center represented the physical body, the heart the emotional body, and the brain the mental body. The brain represented the superior sphere, but after the initiates had passed through the lower degrees they were instructed that the brain was the proxy of the spiritual flame dwelling in the innermost recesses of the heart. The student of esotericism discovers ere long that the ancients often resorted to various blinds to conceal the true interpretations of their Mysteries. The substitution of the brain for the heart was one of these blinds.

The three degrees of the ancient Mysteries were, with few exceptions, given in chambers which represented the three great centers of the human and Universal bodies. If possible, the temple itself was constructed in the form of the human body. The candidate entered between the feet and received the highest degree in the point corresponding to the brain. Thus the first degree was the material mystery and its symbol was the generative system; it raised the candidate through the various degrees of concrete thought. The second degree was given in the chamber corresponding to the heart, but represented the middle power which was the mental link. Here the candidate was initiated into the mysteries of abstract thought and lifted as high as the mind was capable of penetrating. He then passed into the third chamber, which, analogous to the brain, occupied the highest position in the temple but, analogous to the heart, was of the greatest dignity. In the brain chamber the heart mystery was given. Here the initiate for the first time truly comprehended the meaning of those immortal words: "As a man thinketh in his heart, so is he." As there are seven hearts in the brain so there are seven brains in the heart, but this is a matter of superphysics of which little can be said at the present time.

Proclus writes on this subject in the first book of *On the Theology of Plato*: "Indeed, Socrates in the (First) Alcibiades rightly observes, that the soul entering into herself will behold all other things, and deity itself. For verging to her own union, and to the centre of all life, laying aside multitude, and the variety of the all manifold powers which she contains, she ascends to the highest watch-tower offerings. And as in the most holy of the mysteries, they say, that the mystics at first meet with the multi form, and many-shaped genera, which are hurled forth before the gods, but on entering the temple, unmoved, and guarded by the mystic rites, they genuinely receive in their bosom [heart] divine illumination, and divested of their garments, as they would say, participate of a divine nature; the same mode, as it appears to me, takes place in the speculation of wholes. For the soul when looking at things posterior to herself, beholds the shadows and images of beings, but when she converts herself to herself she evolves her own essence, and the reasons which she contains. And at first indeed, she only as it were beholds herself; but, when she penetrates more profoundly into the knowledge of herself, she finds in herself both intellect, and the orders of beings. When however, she proceeds into her interior recesses, and into the adytum as it were of the soul, she perceives with her eye closed [without the aid of the lower mind], the genus of the gods, and the unities of beings. For all things are in us psychically, and through this we are naturally capable of knowing all things, by exciting the powers and the images of wholes which we contain."

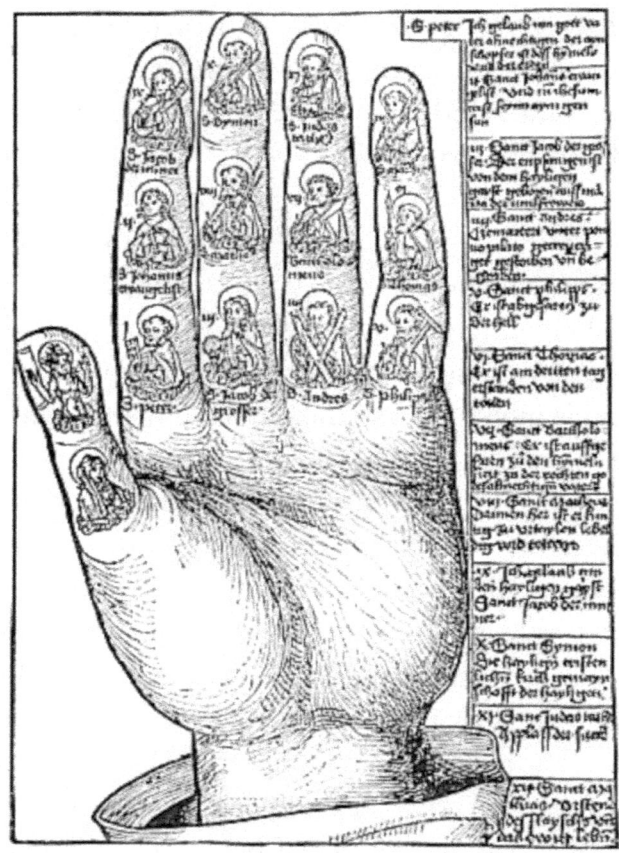

HAND DECORATED WITH EFFIGIES OF JESUS CHRIST, THE VIRGIN MARY, AND THE TWELVE APOSTLES[2]

---

[2] From an old print, courtesy of Carl Oscar Borg.

Upon the twelve phalanges of the fingers, appear the likenesses of the Apostles, each bearing its own appropriate symbol. In the case of those who suffered martyrdom the symbol signifies the instrument of death. Thus, the symbol of St. Andrew is a cross; of St. Thomas, a javelin or a builder's square; of St. James the Less, a club; of St Philip, a cross; of St. Bartholomew, a large knife or scimitar; of St. Matthew, a sword or spear (sometimes a purse); of St. Simon, a club or saw; of St. Matthias, an axe; and of St. Judas, a halbert. The Apostles whose symbols do not elate to their martyrdom are St. Peter, who carries two crossed keys, one gold and one silver; St. James the Great, who bears a pilgrim's staff and an escalop shell; and St. John, who holds a cup from which the poison miraculously departed in the form

The initiates of old warned their disciples that an image is not a reality but merely the objectification of a subjective idea. The image, of the gods were nor designed to be objects of worship but were to be regarded merely as emblems or reminders of invisible powers and principles. Similarly, the body of man must not be considered as the individual but only as the house of the individual, in the same manner that the temple was the House of God. In a state of grossness and perversion man's body is the tomb or principle; in a state of unfoldment and regeneration it is the House or Sanctuary of the Deity by whose creative powers it was fashioned. "Personality is suspended upon a thread from the nature of Being," declares the secret work. Man is essentially a permanent and immortal principle; only his bodies pass through the cycle of birth and death. The immortal is the reality; the mortal is the unreality. During each period of earth life, reality thus dwells in unreality, to be liberated from it temporarily by death and permanently by illumination.

While generally regarded as polytheists, the pagans gained this reputation not because they worshiped more than one God but rather because they personified the attributes of this God, thereby creating a pantheon of posterior deities each manifesting a part of what the One God manifested as a whole. The various pantheons of ancient religions therefore actually represent the catalogued and personified attributes of Deity. In this respect they correspond to the hierarchies of the Hebrew Qabbalists. All the gods and goddesses of antiquity consequently have their analogies in the

---

of a serpent. (See *Handbook of Christian Symbolism*.) The figure of Christ upon the second phalange of the thumb does not follow the pagan system of assigning the first Person of the Creative Triad to this Position. God the Father should occupy the second Phalange, God the Son the first phalange, while to God the Holy Spirit is assigned the base of the thumb.--Also, according to the Philosophic arrangement, the Virgin should occupy the base of the thumb, which is sacred to the moon.

human body, as have also the elements, planets, and constellations which were assigned as proper vehicles for these celestials. Four body centers are assigned to the elements, the seven vital organs to the planets, the twelve principal parts and members to the zodiac, the invisible parts of man's divine nature to various supermundane deities, while the hidden God was declared to manifest through the marrow in the bones.

It is difficult for many to realize that they are actual universes; that their physical bodies are a visible nature through the structure of which countless waves of evolving life are unfolding their latent potentialities. Yet through man's physical body not only are a mineral, a plant, and an animal kingdom evolving, but also unknown classifications and divisions of invisible spiritual life. just as cells are infinitesimal units in the structure of man, so man is an infinitesimal unit in the structure of the universe. A theology based upon the knowledge and appreciation of these relationships is as profoundly just as it is profoundly true.

As man's physical body has five distinct and important extremities--two legs, two arms, and a head, of which the last governs the first four--the number 5 has been accepted as the symbol of man. By its four corners the pyramid symbolizes the arms and legs, and by its apex the head, thus indicating that one rational power controls four irrational corners. The hands and feet are used to represent the four elements, of which the two feet are earth and water, and the two hands fire and air. The brain then symbolizes the sacred fifth element--æther--which controls and unites the other four. If the feet are placed together and the arms outspread, man then symbolizes the cross with the rational intellect as the head or upper limb.

The fingers and toes also have special significance. The toes represent the Ten Commandments of the physical law and the fingers the Ten Commandments of the spiritual law. The four fingers of each hand represent the four elements and the three phalanges of each finger represent the divisions of the element, so that in each hand there are twelve parts to the fingers, which are analogous to the signs of the zodiac, whereas the two phalanges and base of each thumb signify the threefold Deity. The first phalange corresponds to the creative aspect, the second to the preservative aspect, and the base to the generative and destructive aspect. When the hands are brought together, the result is the twenty-four Elders and the six Days of Creation.

In symbolism the body is divided vertically into halves, the right half being considered as light and the left half as darkness. By those unacquainted with the true meanings of light and darkness the light half was denominated spiritual and the left half material. Light is the symbol of objectivity; darkness of subjectivity. Light is a manifestation of life and is therefore posterior to life. That which is anterior to light is darkness, in which light exists temporarily but darkness permanently. As life precedes light, its only symbol is darkness, and darkness is considered as the veil which must eternally conceal the true nature of abstract and undifferentiated Being.

In ancient times men fought with their right arms and defended the vital centers with their left arms, on which was carried the protecting shield. The right half of the body was regarded therefore as offensive and the left half defensive. For this reason also the right side of the body was considered masculine and the left side feminine. Several authorities are of the opinion that the present prevalent right-handedness of the race is the outgrowth of the custom of holding the left hand in restraint for defensive purposes.

Furthermore, as the source of Being is in the primal darkness which preceded light, so the spiritual nature of man is in the dark part of his being, for the heart is on the left side.

Among the curious misconceptions arising from the false practice of associating darkness with evil is one by which several early nations used the right hand for all constructive labors and the left hand for only those purposes termed unclean and unfit for the sight of the gods. For the same reason black magic was often referred to as the left-hand path, and heaven was said to be upon the right and hell upon the left. Some philosophers further declared that there were two methods of writing: one from left to right, which was considered the exoteric method; the other from right to left, which was considered esoteric. The exoteric writing was that which was done out or away from the heart, while the esoteric writing was that which--like the ancient Hebrew--was written toward the heart.

The secret doctrine declares that every part and member of the body is epitomized in the brain and, in turn, that all that is in the brain is epitomized in the heart. In symbolism the human head is frequently used to represent intelligence and self-knowledge. As the human body in its entirety is the most perfect known product of the earth's evolution, it was employed to represent Divinity--the highest appreciable state or condition. Artists, attempting to portray Divinity, often show only a hand emerging from an impenetrable cloud. The cloud signifies the Unknowable Divinity concealed from man by human limitation. The hand signifies the Divine activity, the only part of God which is cognizable to the lower senses.

The face consists of a natural trinity: the eyes representing the spiritual power which comprehends; the nostrils representing the preservative and vivifying power; and the mouth and ears representing the material Demiurgic power of the lower world. The first sphere is eternally existent and is creative; the second sphere pertains to the mystery of the creative breach; and the third sphere to the creative word. By the Word of God the material universe was fabricated, and the seven creative powers, or vowel sounds--which had been brought into existence by the speaking of the Word-- became the seven Elohim or Deities by whose power and ministration the lower world was organized. Occasionally the Deity is symbolized by an eye, an ear, a nose, or a mouth. By the first, Divine awareness is signified; by the second, Divine interest; by the third, Divine vitality; and by the fourth, Divine command.

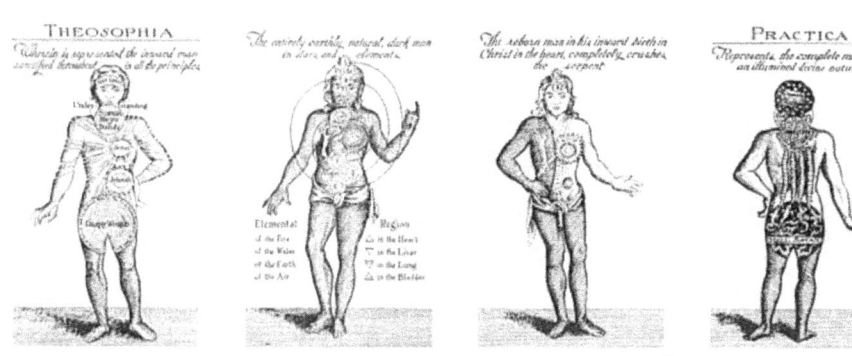

THE THREEFOLD LIFE OF THE INNER MAN[3]

---

[3] Redrawn from Gichtel's *Theosophia Practica*.

Johann Georg Gichtel, a profound Philosopher and mystic, the most illumined of the disciples of Jakob Böhme, secretly circulated the above diagrams among a small group of devoted friends and students. Gichtel republished the writings of Böhme, illustrating them with numerous remarkable figures. According to Gichtel, the diagrams above, represent the anatomy of the divine (or inner) man, and graphically set forth its condition during its human, infernal, and divine states. The plates in the William Law edition of Böhme's works are based apparently upon Gichtel's diagrams, which they follow in all essentials. Gichtel gives no detailed description of his figures, and the lettering on the original diagrams here translated out of the German is the only clue to the interpretation of the charts.

The two end figures represent the obverse and reverse of the same diagram and are termed Table Three. They are "designed to show the Condition of the whole Man, as to all his three essential Parts, Spirit, Soul, and Body, in his Regenerated State." The third figure from the left is called the Second Table, and sets forth "the

The ancients did not believe that spirituality made men either righteous or rational, but rather that righteousness and rationality made men spiritual. The Mysteries taught that spiritual illumination was attained only by bringing the lower nature up to a certain standard of efficiency and purity. The Mysteries were therefore established for the purpose of unfolding the nature of man according to certain fixed rules which, when faithfully followed, elevated the human consciousness to a point where it was capable of cognizing its own constitution and the true purpose of existence. This knowledge of how man's manifold constitution could be most quickly and most completely regenerated to the point of spiritual illumination constituted the secret, or esoteric, doctrine of antiquity. Certain apparently physical organs and centers are in reality the veils or sheaths of spiritual centers. What these were and how they could be unfolded was never revealed to the unregenerate, for the philosophers realized that once he understands the complete working of any system, a man may accomplish a prescribed end without being qualified to manipulate and control the effects which he has produced. For this reason long periods of probation were imposed, so that the knowledge of how to become as the gods might remain the sole possession of the worthy.

Condition of Man in his old, lapsed, and corrupted State; without any respect to, or consideration of his renewing by regeneration." The third figure, however, does not correspond with the First Table of William Law. The First Table presumably represents the condition of humanity before the Fall, but the Gichtel plate pertains to the third, or regenerated, state of mankind. William Law thus describes the purpose of the diagrams, and the symbols upon them: "These three tables are designed to represent Man in his different Threefold State: the First before his Fall, in Purity, Dominion, and Glory: the Second after his Fall, in Pollution and Perdition: and the Third in his rising from the Fall, or on the Way of regeneration, in Sanctification and Tendency to his last Perfection." The student of Orientalism will immediately recognize in the symbols upon the figures the Hindu *chakras*, or centers of spiritual force, the various motions and aspects of which reveal the condition of the disciple's internal divine nature.

Lest that knowledge be lost, however, it was concealed in allegories and myths which were meaningless to the profane but self-evident to those acquainted with that theory of personal redemption which was the foundation of philosophical theology. Christianity itself may be cited as an example. The entire New Testament is in fact an ingeniously concealed exposition of the secret processes of human regeneration. The characters so long considered as historical men and women are really the personification of certain processes which take place in the human body when man begins the task of consciously liberating himself from the bondage of ignorance and death.

The garments and ornamentations supposedly worn by the gods are also keys, for in the Mysteries clothing was considered as synonymous with form. The degree of spirituality or materiality of the organisms was signified by the quality, beauty, and value of the garments worn. Man's physical body was looked upon as the robe of his spiritual nature; consequently, the more developed were his super-substantial powers the more glorious his apparel. Of course, clothing was originally worn for ornamentation rather than protection, and such practice still prevails among many primitive peoples. The Mysteries caught that man's only lasting adornments were his virtues and worthy characteristics; that he was clothed in his own accomplishments and adorned by his attainments. Thus the white robe was symbolic of purity, the red robe of sacrifice and love, and the blue robe of altruism and integrity. Since the body was said to be the robe of the spirit, mental or moral deformities were depicted as deformities of the body.

Considering man's body as the measuring rule of the universe, the philosophers declared that all things resemble in constitution--if not in form--the human body. The Greeks, for example, declared

Delphi to be the navel of the earth, for the physical planet was looked upon as a gigantic human being twisted into the form of a ball. In contradistinction to the belief of Christendom that the earth is an inanimate thing, the pagans considered not only the earth but also all the sidereal bodies as individual creatures possessing individual intelligences. They even went so far as to view the various kingdoms of Nature as individual entities. The animal kingdom, for example, was looked upon as one being--a composite of all the creatures composing that kingdom. This prototypic beast was a mosaic embodiment of all animal propensities and within its nature the entire animal world existed as the human species exists within the constitution of the prototypic Adam.

In the same manner, races, nations, tribes, religions, states, communities, and cities were viewed as composite entities, each made up of varying numbers of individual units. Every community has an individuality which is the sum of the individual attitudes of its inhabitants. Every religion is an individual whose body is made up of a hierarchy and vast host of individual worshipers. The organization of any religion represents its physical body, and its individual members the cell life making up this organism. Accordingly, religions, races, and communities--like individuals--pass through Shakespeare's *Seven Ages*, for the life of man is a standard by which the perpetuity of all things is estimated.

According to the secret doctrine, man, through the gradual refinement of his vehicles and the ever-increasing sensitiveness resulting from that refinement, is gradually overcoming the limitations of matter and is disentangling himself from his mortal coil. When humanity has completed its physical evolution, the empty shell of materiality left behind will be used by other life waves as steppingstones to their own liberation. The trend of man's

THE DIVINE TREE IN MAN
(reverse)[4]

---

[4] From Law's *Figures* of Jakob Böhme.

Just as the diagram representing the front view of man illustrates his divine principles in their regenerated state, so the back view of the same figure sets forth the inferior, or "night," condition of the sun. From the Sphere of the Astral Mind a line ascends through the Sphere of reason into that of the Senses. The Sphere of the evolutionary growth is ever toward his own essential Selfhood. At the point of deepest materialism, therefore, man is at the greatest distance from Himself. According to the Mystery teachings, not all the spiritual nature of man incarnates in matter. The spirit of man is diagrammatically shown as an equilateral triangle with one point downward. This lower point, which is one-third of the spiritual nature but in comparison to the dignity of the other two is much less than a third, descends into the illusion of material existence for a brief space of time. That which never clothes itself in the sheath of matter is the Hermetic *Anthropos*--the Overman-- analogous to the Cyclops or guardian *dæmon* of the Greeks, the *angel* of Jakob Böhme, and the Oversoul of Emerson, "that Unity, that Oversoul, within which every man's particular being is contained and made one with all other."

At birth only a third part of the Divine Nature of man temporarily dissociates itself from its own immortality and takes upon itself the dream of physical birth and existence, animating with its own celestial enthusiasm a vehicle composed of material elements, part of and bound to the material sphere. At death this incarnated part awakens from the dream of physical existence and reunites itself once more with its eternal condition. This periodical descent of spirit into matter is termed the *wheel of life and death*, and the principles involved are treated at length by the philosophers under the subject of metempsychosis. By initiation into the Mysteries and a certain process known as operative theology, this

---

Astral Mind and of the Senses are filled with stars to signify the nocturnal condition of their natures. In the sphere of reason, the superior and the inferior are reconciled, Reason in the mortal man corresponding to Illumined Understanding in the spiritual man.

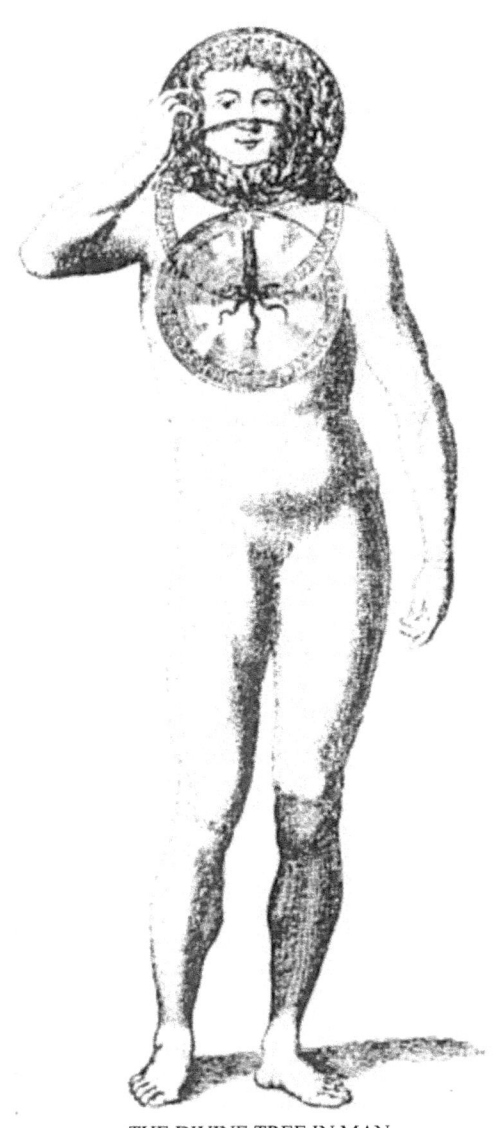

THE DIVINE TREE IN MAN
(obverse)[5]

---

[5] From Law's *Figures* of Jakob Böhme.

A tree with its roots in the heart rises from the Mirror of the Deity through the Sphere of the Understanding to branch forth in the Sphere of the Senses. The roots and trunk of this tree represent the divine nature of man and may be called his *spirituality*; the branches of the tree are the separate parts of the divine constitution and may be likened to the individuality; and the leaves--because of their law of birth and death is transcended, and during the course of physical existence that part of the spirit which is asleep in form is awakened without the intervention of death--the inevitable Initiator--and is consciously reunited with the *Anthropos*, or the overshadowing substance of itself. This is at once the primary purpose and the consummate achievement of the Mysteries: that man shall become aware of and consciously be reunited with the divine source of himself without tasting of physical dissolution.

---

ephemeral nature--correspond to the *personality*, which partakes of none of the permanence of its divine source.

Other Books in this Series and Related Titles

Theosophical Basics by William Q Judge (978–1–63118–608–0)

The Hebrew Talisman by Richard Harte (978–1–63118–607–3)

Early Masonic Symbolism by Manly P Hall (978–1–63118–606–6)

Nature Spirits and Elementals by Louise Off (978-1-63118-605-9)

Swedenborg Bifrons by H P Blavatsky (978-1-63118-604-2)

Practical Use of Psychic Powers by C W Leadbeater (978-1-63118-603-5)

Using White & Black Magic by C W Leadbeater (978-1-63118-602-8)

Jesus, the Last Great Initiate by Edouard Schure (978-1-63118-599-1)

Mysterious Wonders of Antiquity by Manly P Hall (978-1-63118-598-4)

Ancient Mysteries and Secret Societies by Manly P Hall (978–1–63118–597–7)

The Zodiac and Its Signs by Manly P Hall (978–1–63118–596–0)

Life and Teachings of Hermes Trismegistus by Manly P Hall (978–1–63118–595–3)

The Secrets of Doctor Taverner by Dion Fortune (978–1–63118–594–6)

Vegetarianism, Theosophy & Occultism by Leadbeater &c (978–1–63118–593–9)

Applied Theosophy by Henry S Olcott (978–1–63118–592–2)

Higher Consciousness by C W Leadbeater (978–1–63118–591–5)

Theories About Reincarnation and Spirits by H P Blavatsky (978–1–63118–590–8)

The Use and Power of Thought by C W Leadbeater (978–1–63118–589–2)

Commentary on the Pymander by G R S Mead (978–1–63118–588–5)

Hypnotism and Mesmerism by Annie Besant (978–1–63118–587–8)

Spirits of Various Kinds by Helena P Blavatsky (978–1–63118–586–1)

Audio versions are also available on Audible, Amazon and Apple

Other Books in this Series and Related Titles

The Hidden Language of Symbolism by Annie Besant (978–1–63118–585–4)

Eastern Magic & Western Spiritualism by Henry S Olcott (978–1–63118–584–7)

Spiritual Progress and Practical Occultism by H P Blavatsky (978–1–63118–583–0)

Memory and Consciousness by Besant & Blavatsky (978–1–63118–582–3)

The Origin of Evil by Helena P Blavatsky (978–1–63118–581–6)

The Camp of Philosophy: Studies in Alchemy by Bloomfield (978–1–63118–580–9)

The Testaments of the Twelve Patriarchs (978–1–63118–579–3)

Occult or Exact Science? by Helena P Blavatsky (978–1–63118–578–6)

Occultism, Semi-Occultism & Pseudo Occultism by A Besant (978–1–63118–577–9)

The Fourth-Gospel and Synoptical Problem by G R S Mead (978–1–63118–576–2)

On the Bhagavad-Gita by T Subba Row &c (978–1–63118–575–5)

What Theosophy Does for Us by C W Leadbeater (978–1–63118–574–8)

Spiritual Life for Man by Annie Besant (978–1–63118–573–1)

The Mysteries by Annie Besant (978–1–63118–572–4)

Fundamental Ideas of Theosophy by Bhagwan Das (978–1–63118–571–7)

Dreams: What They Are and How They Are Caused (978–1–63118–570–0)

Communication Between Different Worlds by Annie Besant (978–1–63118–569–4)

Animism, Magic and the Omnipotence of Thought by S Freud (978–1–63118–568–7)

Buddhism by F Otto Schrader (978–1–63118–567–0)

Death by W W Westcott (978–1–63118–566–3)

The Religion of Theosophy by Bhagwan Das (978–1–63118–565–6)

Audio versions are also available on Audible, Amazon and Apple

www.ingramcontent.com/pod-product-compliance
Lightning Source LLC
LaVergne TN
LVHW041503070426
835507LV00009B/798